Times Table

Time

&

Rhyme

Terrifying Times Tables

Christopher Davies

For Izzy,
my super-special sister.
Thanks for all your support.

Times Table Time

&

Rhyme

'Terrifying Times Tables' is the second title in the 'Times Table Time & Rhyme' series, created by Chris Davies.

Chris has over twenty five years experience of teaching primary mathematics and knows how important it is for children to learn their times tables at an early age, for developing confidence and a love of maths.

Chris has worked with primary aged children to develop and test out his latest book of rhymes, which helps children to learn their times tables in a fun and interactive way.

Thank you

I would like to say a big thank you to my editing team (MAC, JMCD, BCD and RCD) for their help and feedback in the development of the rhymes and a special thank you to Megan for her creative support with the illustrations and design.

I would also like to say a huge thank you to my 'Junior Reading Maths Group' (Finlay, Halle, Leen, Mohammed, Josh, Hamish and George) for all their constructive feedback and ideas.

Special thanks to Pixabay for allowing me to use some of their amazing images and especially to Judy, at Kenilworth Books, for all her generous help and advice with sales and marketing.

Finally, I would like to say a massive, big thank you to you the reader for buying this book. I hope you enjoy reading the rhymes and that they help you to learn your times tables.

CONTENTS

Top Tips for Times Table Learners

(Message to children, parents, carers, grandparents and teachers)

1) To achieve the best rhythm for the rhymes, I suggest reading the **numbers** as follows:

> "**One 2 is 2** – Pinky Pranky Pooh"
>
> "**Two 2's are 4** – Stink bombs hit the floor!"
>
> "**Three 2's are 6** – Smart and smelly tricks"

This will help create a quicker pace to the rhyme, which will make it read better and help make it easier to learn.

"One times 2 is 2, Two times 2 is 4," will also work well but PLEASE DO NOT USE, "One times 2 equals 2, Two times 2 equals 4…", as this will slow the rhythm down too much.

2) You can be read the rhymes on your own, but they will also work very well if reading with a parent, grandparent, sibling or friend. When reading with a partner, sometimes **you** could read **just the numbers** and your partner could read the **corresponding rhyme**.

For example, you read, "One 2 is 2," and they read, "Pinky Pranky Pooh"

Then you read, "Two 2's are 4," and they read, "Stink bombs hit the floor!"

Then you read, "Three 2's are 6," and they read, "Smart and smelly tricks"

This will help **you** to really focus on the **number pattern** of the **times table**. After a while swap over and let your partner read the numbers and you can read the corresponding rhyme. Before long you will know your times tables off by heart!

3) Reading the rhymes **in reverse** can also be fun and help you learn:

> "There's an alien at the door! - One 4 is 4"
>
> "And HUNDREDS by the gate! – Two 4's are 8"

I hope you have hours of fun reading these rhymes and learning your times tables together.

Terrifying Times Table Challenge

Ready to challenge yourself? When you are trying to recall your times table from memory, the rhymes can be used to help you to remember the correct answer. For example, if you are stuck on 6 x 6 = ? Your reading partner can read the next line of the rhyme – "Daring moves and clever tricks!" You will then know that the answer you need rhymes with 'tricks'. Using the rhyme as clues will make learning your times tables more fun and interactive. This will also help speed up your learning.

Chilling Challenge Cup &
Terrifying Times Table Champion

At the back of the book you will have the chance to put your times table knowledge to the test! You will be asked to answer multiple times table facts in a short period of time. Can you win the 'Chilling Challenge Cup' or become a 'Terrifying Times Table Champion?' I'm sure you can. Good luck!

x2   Pinky Pranky Pooh

1 x 2 = 2	Pinky Pranky Pooh
2 x 2 = 4	Stink bombs hit the floor!
3 x 2 = 6	Smart and smelly tricks
4 x 2 = 8	Roll the marbles - wait...
5 x 2 = 10	Slips and trips – MAYHEM!
6 x 2 = 12	In Miss's desk we delve...
7 x 2 = 14	Hide a toad all warty green...
8 x 2 = 16	SLIMY, croaking – quite obscene!
9 x 2 = 18	When she sees it... WHAT a SCREAM!
10 x 2 = 20	Miss is in a FRENZY!
11 x 2 = 22	The HEAD is coming! Didn't think this through..
12 x 2 = 24	We've gone and booby-trapped the door!!!

x3   Haunted House

1 x 3 = 3	So sick and SCAREEE!
2 x 3 = 6	Shockingly SPOOKY tricks!
3 x 3 = 9	HAUNTING TIME!!!
4 x 3 = 12	It's DARK - all by ourselves...
5 x 3 = 15	Suddenly... a frightful scream!
6 x 3 = 18	Vampires, ZOMBIES – ghastly scene!
7 x 3 = 21	Ghosts... ghouls.. and a SKELETON!
8 x 3 = 24	Trap door opens – in we FALL!
9 x 3 = 27	Terror grips us – pray to heaven!
10 x 3 = 30	"PLEASE... don't hurt me!"
11 x 3 = 33	At last day light, fresh air – we're FREE!
12 x 3 = 36	But a WITCH above our head still flits...

x4   Alien Attack

1 x 4 = 4   There's an alien at the door!

2 x 4 = 8   And HUNDREDS by the gate!

3 x 4 = 12   RUN and SAVE yourselves!!

4 x 4 = 16   Skull-shaped heads, four legs all green.

5 x 4 = 20   Screams of TERROR – PLENTY!

6 x 4 = 24   Menacing, marching... dressed for WAR!

7 x 4 = 28   How on EARTH can we escape?!

8 x 4 = 32   Hiding in the upstairs loo...

9 x 4 = 36   Will they cut us into BITS...?

10 x 4 = 40   This could end up GORY...

11 x 4 = 44   Through the door they start to saw...

12 x 4 = 48   The door flies off – we stare and gape....

x5   Cruel-Kid Clive

1 x 5 = 5	Wanted DEAD or ALIVE…
2 x 5 = 10	He's hid up in his den…
3 x 5 = 15	The MEANEST outlaw ever seen!
4 x 5 = 20	Shooting, looting plenty!
5 x 5 = 25	Out in a posse, we did ride…
6 x 5 = 30	Folks say he fights REAL dirty!
7 x 5 = 35	Trapped like a rat – he can't survive…
8 x 5 = 40	His face so SLY and swarthy
9 x 5 = 45	"No mistaking… it's Cruel-Kid Clive!"
10 x 5 = 50	Bullets blasting – RISKY!
11 x 5 = 55	"QUICK! He's snuck out on the other side…"
12 x 5 = 60	"HOW did he 'doggone' get FREE?!"

[Read this rhyme in an American accent for added effect!]

x6 Dangerous Dancing

1 x 6 = 6	The B-kids music mix
2 x 6 = 12	Just doing it for themselves
3 x 6 = 18	The UK's top break-dancing team!
4 x 6 = 24	Hip-hop, rap and much, much more
5 x 6 = 30	Beat box BLARES absurdly!
6 x 6 = 36	Daring moves and clever kicks
7 x 6 = 42	Wheeling windmills – whizzing through!
8 x 6 = 48	Awesome head spin! Sick - first-rate!
9 x 6 = 54	Hand Hops, Bronco's - we want more!
10 x 6 = 60	MESMERISING – TRICKSY!
11 x 6 = 66	Flying front-flip – flares and flicks!
12 x 6 = 72	Crowd go CRAZY – cries of WHOO!!!!

x7   Hell or Heaven?

1 x 7 = 7	Breaking the BEAST at Sennen!
2 x 7 = 14	The wickedest waves you've ever seen!
3 x 7 = 21	Waiting for a GIGANTIC one...
4 x 7 = 28	Missed it! Bother! Just too late!
5 x 7 = 35	WOW! I've caught one! What a RIDE!
6 x 7 = 42	Whizzing through the water – WHOO!
7 x 7 = 49	Frightening-Exciting at the VERY same time!
8 x 7 = 56	Now to do some 'cool-dude' tricks...
9 x 7 = 63	'WOWS' and 'WIPEOUTS' – Cries of glee!
10 x 7 = 70	This is hellish but mostly heavenly!
11 x 7 = 77	Surfing at Sennen is our new 'seventh heaven'
12 x 7 = 84	Spray, spills and thrills and a rapturous ROAR!

(Sennen Cove is a fantastic surfing beach near Lands End, Cornwall.)

x8 Gaming Glory

1 x 8 = 8	Gaming very late…
2 x 8 = 16	Lonely landscape – monsters MEAN!
3 x 8 = 24	Survivors of a storm before…
4 x 8 = 32	Snipers sniping – missed us – PHEW!
5 x 8 = 40	Last team standing – GLORY!
6 x 8 = 48	Fearsome forts we scavenge and make…
7 x 8 = 56	Hope we don't get blown to bits…
8 x 8 = 64	Ninja's closing – rockets ROAR!
9 x 8 = 72	HELP ! I'm injured! Where are you…?
10 x 8 = 80	I'm coming to save you, Jakey!
11 x 8 = 88	Grenades away… Take cover, mate!
12 x 8 = 96	What a WIN! Let's get some chips!

x9   Deadly Dentist

1 x 9 = 9   Deadly dentist time…

2 x 9 = 18   Wish I'd flossed and kept them clean…

3 x 9 = 27   Please go gentle – I'm just eleven!

4 x 9 = 36   A HUGE sharp needle in my mouth he sticks!

5 x 9 = 45   They say not many come out ALIVE…

6 x 9 = 54   He's like a MONSTER in a film I saw!

7 x 9 = 63   Hands like CLAWS – hair WILD and free!

8 x 9 = 72   ALONE with a WEREWOLF… what can I do?!

9 x 9 = 81   He's … TRANSFORMING! I want to RUN!!!

10 x 9 = 90   His howl is FOUL and WINEY!

11 x 9 = 99   The moon is up and so's my TIME…

12 x 9 =108   "You're finished," he smiles. "See you next

                 time, Kate…."

x10   Fight for the Flag

1 x 10 = 10   Let's get to it then!

2 x 10 = 20   CHARGE! Let's give them PLENTY!

3 x 10 = 30   Red team's fighting DIRTY!

4 x 10 = 40   Watch your back – it's Shorty!

5 x 10 = 50   She is super-shifty!

6 x 10 = 60   Dodging pellets …NIFTY!

7 x 10 = 70   Our guns are running empty…

8 x 10 = 80   We're coming! WAKEY! WAKEY!

9 x 10 = 90   Sprinting – shooting blindly…

10 x 10 = 100   Our days are looking numbered…

11 x 10 = 110   Their FLAG! It's FALLEN… we've WON again!

12 x 10 = 120   Cheering, laughter - high-fives aplenty!

X11   Jump Jitters

1 x 11 = 11   Time for my leap from heaven!

2 x 11 = 22   PETRIFIED – my nails I chew...

3 x 11 = 33   Hope I don't end up in a tree!

4 x 11 = 44   SHAKING... QUAKING... we await our call...

5 x 11 = 55   Doors spring open – out we DIVE!

6 x 11 = 66   HELTER-SKELTER – my life just flicks...

7 x 11 = 77   Wish that I'd gone, on that fishing trip to Devon!

8 x 11 = 88   Plunging perilously to our fate....

9 x 11 = 99   Will it open... SOON... in time... ??!

10 x 11 = 110   I'm sure it will, but when, when... WHEN?!

11 x 11 = 121   WHOOSH!! Now I'm gliding... this is almost kind of FUN!

12 x 11 = 132   Not sure where I'm landing yet... hope it's not the Wildcat Zoo?!!!

x12   Marine Monster

1 x 12 = 12	Into the depths we delve...
2 x 12 = 24	Searching for secrets on the ocean floor
3 x 12 = 36	Sinister silence – heart beat quicks...
4 x 12 = 48	What hidden DANGERS lie in wait..?
5 x 12 = 60	Rugged wreck – all twisty
6 x 12 = 72	Schools of fish - green, red and blue
7 x 12 = 84	Then out of the gloom... a JAGGED JAW!
8 x 12 = 96	DEADLY monster - that KILLS for kicks!!
9 x 12 = 108	Flipping madly – in panic state!
10 x 12 = 120	Oxygen tanks are almost empty...
11 x 12 = 132	Our boat at last! We made it - PHEW!
12 x 12 = 144	I've never been so close to a GREAT WHITE SHARK before!

Glossary

blares	~	*loud, harsh sound*
delve	~	*reach inside, search*
doggone	~	*darn it (annoyed)*
fate	~	*destiny, written in stars*
flits	~	*fly quickly*
folks	~	*people*
frenzy	~	*hysterical outburst*
gape	~	*stare, open-mouthed*
glory	~	*honour won, fame*
helter-skelter	~	*at full speed*

mayhem	~	*chaos, madhouse*
mesmerising	~	*spellbinding, dazzling*
outlaw	~	*wanted criminal*
perilously	~	*great danger, risk*
posse	~	*a group of men, cowboys*
rapturous	~	*overjoyed, happy*
snuck out	~	*sneaked out*
swarthy	~	*dark/tanned skin*
tricksy	~	*ingenious, complicated*
wipeout	~	*fall from a surf board*

Dear Reader

I hope you enjoyed this book. If you did, please leave me a book review on amazon.co.uk. – I would be very interested in hearing from you. Which rhymes and illustrations did you like the best? Has it helped you to learn your times tables? I hope it has!

How much progress have you made? Have you won the 'Chilling Challenge Cup' or become a 'Terrifying Times Table Champion' or 'Super-Spooky Champion'?

Keep an eye out for my next book in the series which will be out later in 2020.

Best wishes

Christopher Davies

Chilling Challenge Cup

Are you ready to test your times table knowledge and try and win the Challenge Cup? If so, photocopy this grid and see how many you can get right in 10 minutes. The first row is the 10 times table - I have filled in a few answers to help you. Can you **score 132 out of 132** and win the **Chilling Challenge Cup**? After each attempt fill in the Date, Time, Score and Target.* (see page 29) **Good luck! You can do it!**

X	1	2	3	4	5	6	7	8	9	10	11	12
10	10	20	30									
5	5	10										
2												
4												
3												
6												
7												
8												
9												
11												
12												

Date		Score		Time		Target	

Terrifying Times Table Challenge

Are you ready for an even trickier times table challenge? Can you score 100 out of 100 in less than 8 minutes and become a **'Terrifying Times Table Champion'**?

1) Photocopy this grid & put in 10 numbers from 1 - 12 in a **random** order across the top row. E.g. 2,4,5,3,6,9,7,8,12,11. The first number has been put in for you and the answer 10 x 2 = **20**

2) Give yourself 8 minutes to complete as many as you can – no peeping in the book please!

3) Get some help to check your answers and record your score out of 100 and the time and date.

4) To work out your new **Target**, just add on 10. If you scored 45, your new target will be 55. If you score 100 in 8 minutes try and beat your time by 10 seconds and so on. If you score 100 out of 100 in less than 6 minutes you will become a ... **'Terrifying Times Table Super-Spooky Champ'?!**

x	2									
10	20									
5										
2										
4										
3										
6										
7										
9										
8										
12										
Date			Score			Time		Target		

Books by Christopher Davies

If you would like to find out about (or purchase) other books written by the author, please visit Kenilworth Books or check out the Author's Page for Christopher Davies on amazon.co.uk

Books available include:

'Transformer the Tiger Cat'

A humorous adventure about a boy who keeps changing things! Connor's peculiar habit gets him into all sorts of trouble, but things get even worse when he makes a birthday wish to turn his pet tabby cat into a tiger… Age 6+

Times Table Time and Rhyme

Catchy amusing rhymes to help make learning your

Times Tables....

EASY & ENJOYABLE!

Popular themes include: snow, football, the seaside, baking a cake, sports day, trips to the zoo & the school disco.

Read aloud with family & friends!

Hours of FUN...

and... LEARNING!   Age 5+

'I use this book with my Year 2 class and they absolutely love it! They are so keen to learn their times tables now. A fantastic book to engage all children and get them learning.' Ms Nunn (teacher)

Prickly-Pong Island
and the
Emerald Treasure

TREASURE is a wonderful thing... but is it more important than anything?

Jay finds school difficult but his twin sister Sanjana loves it - so when Dad wins a holiday to a desert island, Jay thinks all his dreams have come true! Maths and spellings tests are happily replaced with climbing palm trees and making friends with the mischievous monkeys.

But living in an island paradise doesn't turn out to be all fun & games and before long, Jay and Sanjana become entangled in a daring real-life escapade they would never have believed possible! Pirates and 'Prickly-Pong' - lost treasure and tattooed tribes. Life soon becomes VERY different from school! Danger is lurking everywhere - something far more terrifying than the most menacing pirate...

A thrilling 'green-themed' adventure set in the islands of the South-Pacific. Full of humour & happiness; sadness & regret; bravery & friendship. 7+

"My 7 year old son absolutely loved this story... A perfect mix of adventure and suspense. He didn't want it to end and can't wait for the next one in the series." Lucy

In a Spin

It's almost time! The annual St. George's Dance Competition is only days away. Maddy is favourite to win but something serious is bothering her...

Close friend, Jack is a daring Break-Dancer who is going all out to beat his arch rival Justin, but will Jack's fiery temper get the better of him?

All the twists and turns you could wish for in this lively, action-packed, School Dance drama.   Age 8+

"This book is amazing. After reading the first couple of chapters I wanted to read all of it straight away! The character of Maddy is my favourite as she loves dancing like me and I like the end of term dance competition... I loved the ending because it was surprising. I would give it loads more than 5 stars if I could!"   Lottie (Age 9)

Printed in Great Britain
by Amazon